Making Traveling FUN

by Michele Spirn
Illustrated by Nuri Vergara

Scott Foresman
is an imprint of

Glenview, Illinois • Boston, Massachusetts • Chandler, Arizona •
Upper Saddle River, New Jersey

Illustrations
Nuri Vergara

ISBN 13: 978-0-328-50847-1
ISBN 10:   0-328-50847-0

5 6 7 8 9 10 V010 13 12

Have you ever traveled on a long car trip? Sometimes a trip can be long and boring. Other times it can be fun. What makes the difference? You have to plan for fun!

You also need some good ideas. Here are ideas that helped Joe and Ann have the perfect trip.

Using Your Imagination

They each gathered a blanket and some pillows. They made the back seat into a cave. Then, they used the pillows to divide the space in half.

Joe and Ann had fun. They each had their own little clearing.

Drinks

Joe brought their favorite drinks for the trip. He put orange juice into a small bottle with a cap. A straw keeps the juice from splashing or spilling when the car is moving.

Snacks

Ann helped Mom pack snacks. They packed things such as carrots, cheese, crackers, and fruit.

Ann was careful about the fruit she packed. She didn't want soft fruit with pits. They can be messy to handle. She packed fruit such as apples and grapes instead.

Toys

Joe and Ann knew it would be a long ride to their grandparent's house. That's why they packed some of their favorite books and toys.

On one trip, toys crashed to the floor of the car. Some of them broke. Some got lost. On this trip, they didn't pack toys with lots of pieces.

Things to Do

The children also brought a map of the places they were going. As they drove, they searched for things they saw on the map. They looked for rivers and ponds.

Then, as they drove through towns, they checked them off on the map. They guessed how long it would take to get from one town to another.

Games

Joe and Ann also played games. They had fun counting things. They counted all the red cars. They counted the motels they passed.

They played guessing games too. They asked Mom and Dad to guess which person or animal they were thinking of. Then Joe and Ann gave them clues. Mom and Dad never guessed right!

The next time you take a long car trip, try some of these ideas. You can also come up with your own ideas.

Ann and Joe know if you plan ahead, you'll have more fun and your trip will go faster!